The Importance of
DISCIPLINE

Dr. Ruth Davis

TABLE OF CONTENTS

INTRODUCTION

*"Whoever practices **DISCIPLINE** is on the way to life..."*

-Proverbs 10:17

One of the foundations of living a prosperous and fulfilling life is to find and exercise inner strength. Discipline is life and crown jewel of "Free will." It is the distinction and privilege of human life.

I'm glad you finally laid your hands on this life-transforming book. Get ready to be informed and equipped to live beyond failure and vain excuses. I am going to let you in on the place and power of self-discipline. The truth is, you cannot rise beyond the horizon of adequate knowledge. Surely, ignorance is lethal.

This book has been carefully written to reflect beams of light that will expose the activities of the enemy that seeks to keep you locked out of the purpose and plan of God for your life. I am passionate about letting you realize the importance and discover the benefits of natural and spiritual discipline.

*"I correct and **DISCIPLINE** everyone I love.*

Take this seriously

and change the way you think and act."

-Revelations 3:19

Certainly, it takes discipline to walk with God and sacrifice to remain steady on the path of spiritual progress. You cannot please God without faith in His word and faithfulness to keep his commands. Going by feelings and comfort instead of faith and self-control is a recipe for disaster.

Nothing worthwhile can be achieved outside diligent, principled, committed, and consistent actions towards an envisioned goal or identified objective. A man or woman who is led and ruled by pleasure and mere affinity for frivolities will not be able to make progress in life.

So, it is time to say No! Not every attraction is a green light for action. We need to start measuring up to higher standards for life at work, school, home, and every other place. This book will be a companion and guide from where you are as regards inner strength to where 4

God wants you to be through attempts to harness your God-given potential for personal-restraint.

Often times, individuals, Organizations, and Nations are acquainted with steps to be taken, action plans to follow and goals that need to be achieved to take them from where they are to where they need to be. However, only a few are free from the limitations of their decisions to relegate personal restraint.

Discipline is the trait of being well behaved, based on certain principles or methods of practice. Where there are no guiding principles, disorderliness will prevail. If control is taken from any circle of life, chaos will be the inevitable outcome. No one should act irrationally and do things without putting others into consideration.

Rainfall, snow, ocean, Sun and moon, and several creatures function by the laws and principles that established their creation. If there happens to be any violation of these measures of control, the results are often fatal and destructive. Discipline brings beauty to life and order to all creation.

Where there are no guiding principles, disorderliness is the other of the day. If there were no discipline in any circle of life, one would act irrationally and do things without putting others into consideration.

Every professional athlete recognizes the place of self-denial for strenuous training that must come before any trophy. There are certain rules and guidelines they must stick to be at their best. There are diets that must be avoided and pleasures that must be denied.

Likewise, music, entertainment, invention, business, and every other facet of life requires commitment and consistency before any praiseworthy performance, achievement, fulfillment, and success.

"We don't enjoy being disciplined. It always seems to cause more pain than joy. But later on, those who learn from that discipline have peace that comes from doing what is right."

-Hebrews 12:11

This book will utilize contemporary and Biblical examples to help you discover role models who led a life of self-control and identify the pitfalls of lack of discipline through the errors of those who lived without an appropriate appreciation of commitment to personal restraint.

You will find that the first chapter of this book will help you become aware of your true identity and the need for discipline in your life based on divine and temporal demands on your destiny for genuine meaning and positive manifestation.

Chapter two will introduce you to the realities and implications of times and seasons in your life. This realization will help you attain consciousness of where you are in divine mandate and timing as it relates to the ever-increasing need for discipline in every stage of your life.

Chapter three will expose the enemies within. Ego and complacency will be revealed as great hindrances to a life of self-control. You will discover how ego and complacency often try to take control of life for destruction.

Chapter 4 will help you detect and minimize wastage. You will find several destiny wasters, understand their lethal strategy against your life and strength to minimize or eradicate their influence over your life.

In Chapter 5, you will learn to keep your eyes on the prize. You will learn how to remain disciplined enough to avoid distractions on your path to spiritual and natural accomplishments.

Chapter 6 will inspire you to keep on going when things get tough and equally equip you with things to do when everything seems not to go as you have expected.

Finally, in chapter 7, you will acquire various ways to leverage God divine advantage amidst trial of life.

Once more, I say, congratulation for getting this book and I assure you that it will be a life changing experience!

CHAPTER 1

THE POWER OF AWARENESS

"But ye are a chosen generation, a royal priesthood, a holy nation, a peculiar people; that ye should shew forth the praises of him who hath called you out of darkness into his marvelous light: "

-1 Peter 2:9

"Awareness is the greatest agent for change."

-Eckhart Tolle

Your perception about life and who you are will reflect on attitude and determine your progress in life. If you are to rise to become who you can be and all that you are in Christ, then recognizing who you are, as being a peculiar person is just the beginning.

To grow your inner strength, you need to identify and focus on the reality of who you truly are in Christ.

Salvation in Jesus always transforms us from who we used to be to a brand new person on a spiritual level. We have become like God! If you are born again, you are different, disciplined, and blessed; even though you may not seem to live in these realities due to ignorance.

Every believer in Jesus has been set apart for something spectacular. We have been endowed on the inside with the necessary skills, discipline, talents, and thoughts that do not exist under the shadows of natural limitations. This makes us stand out as an individual

" The ultimate value of life depends upon awareness and the power of contemplation rather than upon mere survival."

-Aristotle

Welcome to the first chapter of this book. I am certain that your life will begin to move in the right direction from here. There is a chance that this book is in your hands because you care about your progress with God and life.

You may be sick and tired of being sick and tired. You might be suffering from poor decisions of loose and excuse-filled living. You might have gained too much weight, lost your job, spouse, family, career, or unique opportunities for lack of discipline.

On the other hand, the truth is, you may think you are on the right and bright side of life, nothing seems to be out of place, and your decisions have often been spot on. Well, I must say that I'm happy for you if you feel this way.

However, I'm sure that you still need the valuable information in this book. Wisdom is found in humility to learn. You might need another reminder or probably an awakening to areas that your life has fallen behind the purpose and plan of God for your experience in this realm of existence.

Welcome to the chapter that seeks to help you make discoveries and bring you helpful and timely realization of who you were, who you are and who you have been designed to become in the light of discipline and the life in God's word.

Let there be LIGHT!

"And God said, Let there be light: and there was light..."

-**Genesis 1:3**

Discovery is the first step to recovery. You must become informed to get transformed. No lasting change can come without a deep sense of illumination and awareness of issues in the past, present situation, and future aspirations.

On the glorious morning of creation, before anything was made. The whole Earth was no more than a mass of chaos, filled with darkness and void of life.

The Spirit of God swung into action to bring beauty and life into the world. The first thing God did was to create possibility for vision through the brightness of the light. This first and strategic move still applies to every form of meaningful creation and life restoration today. It is pertinent that we find light as we turn the beams of sober reflection and personal assessment in every corner of our heart and life.

This is the first place to begin if we must appreciate our situation and understand the necessity and realize the urgency of a lasting change. The inner strength that produces self-control must be discovered through adequate attention to details about our inner self and issues that surround our life.

Awareness of your situation

"Examine yourselves…"

-2 Corinthians 13:5

The greatest discovery one can ever make is self-discovery. Every soul that desires and aspires for greater height must be aware of his position and limitation in any situation. If you have no clear clue or idea of who you are, you will have no clarity in what you want or seek. Just as Deepak Chopra once said, *"The key to transforming your life is to be aware of who you are."* How much do you know about your family background? What are the principles they uphold that are working for them or against them? What are those past experiences that have formed your perception about life and how you relate with everyone and everything? Are you not stepping into the same principles, lifestyle, or ideologies that brought people in your life to that position you find them today?

The current situation you found yourself now is based on a certain decision you have made or neglected in the past. You need time to think clearly about the questions I have asked and generate even more relevant questions that will help you find the root of the kind of attitude, lifestyle and perception that you have adopted for life and be able to connect them to your present situation (Good or Bad!).

Critically examine yourself and your life and know where you stand in the spectrum of self-control.

"Oh, how I hated discipline! How my heart despised correction!"

-Proverbs 5:12

It is pertinent to ascertain why you engage in some activities, and you restrain from others. Are your actions based on other's reaction, fleeting emotions, or clearly understood principles for effective living?

Are you conscious of your daily activities or habits? Are you able to discern what you should do rather what you want to do or compelled to do?

It is very necessary to ask yourself where you are when it comes to living in obedience or rebellion, order or chaos, the principle of loose pleasure correction or error. This will help you ascertain the things you need to change and how to make those critical changes.

Majority of people today tend to conform to the certain rules and regulations because of the punishments that are attached to them. They live their life based on the fear of the laws without paying adequate attention to beliefs and ideas that make it hard to stick to the right path and follow wholesome principles. Discipline must be cultivated even without fear of punishment.

Any discipline without inner conviction is like a time bomb waiting to explode. Self-discipline makes you do what you ought to do with or without the external compulsion or investigation.

Without discipline, you will be used, pushed, and pulled by the desires of the other people and by the irrational whims of your own.

Many opportunities that are lost today or failures that are encountered are probably as a result of not yielding to instructions. The bible says, "Poverty and shame are for those who ignore correction, but whoever listens to instruction gains honor."(Proverb 13:18) Entrepreneurs who neglect the place of discipline in any endeavor should equally be prepared for the sad outcome. Families and relationships that ought to be paradise on earth have become a shadow of itself due to lack of discipline. A professional that lack discipline will lose his reputation and sometimes his entire career.

Therefore, you have to vividly find areas in your life that lack of discipline has left an indelible mark on your personality and circumstances.

Awareness of God's mandate on your life

"You are… chosen …that [will] show forth the praises of Him who has called you out of darkness into His marvelous light…"

-Philippians 2:9b

Everything that God created is for an assigned purpose. The purpose is to give God glory. So, whatever brings beauty, order, and praise to God is actually fulfilling the purpose of its creation. Your life will give God glory when you walk outside the realm of excuses for failure into a new level of personal resolve to act according to principles that may appear stringent but promises life and success.

There is no mistake or error in all of God's creation; you will not be the first. He gave every individual the mandate and the power to dominate, to have full control over themselves and all of creation.

However, without the divine purpose and direction in any life, an effort to sustain discipline and inner strength for noble resolve will become bouts of endless struggle and frustration.

Truthfully, before the universe was created, God already knew everything about us in great intimate detail, In the book of Jeremiah, He made his intention known when he said that

"Before I formed thee in the belly I knew thee, and before thou camest forth out of the womb, I sanctified thee, and I ordained thee a prophet unto the nations."

-Jeremiah 1:5

He endows us with a specific personality and gifts to fulfill our divine assignment on earth. You see, once we surrender our lives to him, it is then that he can truly begin to transform us into what he had already proposed and purposed in our lives.

In conclusion, where you are today is an outcome of decisions of your past; likewise, your future is being molded by the steps you take today. Don't lay down this book until you have adequately examined your life in the mirror of your stand with God and experiences in life.

Stop making excuses and get serious…! Turn on the light and you will see that redemption is here.

CHAPTER 2

UNDERSTAND
TIMES AND
SEASONS

"*To everything, there is a season, and a time for every purpose under the heavens:*"

-Ecclesiastes 3:1

Nothing in the universe happens by chance without a process. There is a process and purpose for every form of existence, and every purpose has its timing. Right from the creation, God has determined there would be times and seasons.

This was why He made the sun, moon, and stars to provide information and signs about times and seasons. They were created to give light to the day (Sun) and give light to the Night (the moon), everything operates based on the way it has been placed and the command given by the creator. The day will pave the way for the night similarly, the night will give place to the day as the cycle continues in perfect order and harmony.

Surely, discipline is required to exercise patience at the moment, knowing that success must take time. Sadly, many people have missed their time of manifestation today due to indiscipline. They find it difficult to delay their gratification and have engaged in diverse careless and costly activities during their waiting season.

Interestingly, only a few can comprehend or accept the possibility of being on the right and bright side of times and seasons of life. To the undisciplined people, time is the greatest enemy; there are the anxiety and curiosity to desire quick fix or complain about the due process.

This chapter will focus on three distinct effects of indiscipline about time. You will realize that; indiscipline will make it difficult for you to wait patiently for your time, it will make you to miss your time and finally and it will eventually prolong your waiting season.

Indiscipline will make it hard to wait for the right time

Today, several people are in a hurry to get wealth and find success in different areas of their lives without regard for principles and processes that birth greatness. Therefore, undisciplined people are prone to impatience that rushes them to make rash decisions, careless actions, and several corrupt practices.

Unfortunately, little do they understand that there is always a season for happy endings after times of humble beginnings. Some have moved hastily from their place of glorification to find destruction, rushed from a place of honor to shame and drift from a place of grace to condemnation; only because they lack regard for the appropriate times and seasons of life.

The irony of this is that blessings, wealth and fame they clamor for are on their way to find them but their lack of discipline and will-power to wait for their appointed time have caused them immeasurable loss.

Examples of people that cannot wait for their time of glory

Have you ever met Gehazi...?

The name Gehazi might sound very unfamiliar to you. But, the Bible narrates the story of a servant to Elisha, a more popular Prophet in the Old Testament. Gehazi was the servant of Prophet Elisha, as Elisha was also the servant of another Top Prophet named

Elijah, who handed down the anointing and power to Elisha.

Gehazi was supposed to be the next in line, but indiscipline and love of money ruined his Prophetic career. Even though, Gehazi seemed to have started quite well, yet, he could not reign as a prophet when his time came to enter that noble office.

Interestingly, Gehazi followed Elisha all the way to carry out several divine assignments and was supposed to take over the ministry after his death just as Elisha took over from Elijah. 14 Although, Gehazi saw how Elisha performed diverse miracles and how he stood up against the corrupt Kings in his days. He never learned discipline and leadership. He was always driven by what he felt he needed instead of taking responsibility for his actions and wait patiently through the making process.

One day, a powerful Syrian Army General called Naaman was introduced to Elisha because he needed healing for leprosy. This was a stigma and reproach that limited Naaman in several ways, even though he was rich and powerful.

Fortunately, Naaman got healed by following divine instructions from Prophet Elisha, and he rightly felt the need to show some appreciation. He brought gifts in gold and garments to the prophet and healer. However, for some reasons, Elisha refused to collect anything from Naaman.

Indiscipline mixed with rebellion rose within the heart of Gehazi, and he was displeased by his master's refusal of Naman's gifts. This eventually made Gehazi hit the road to go after Naaman so he can find a way to collect the gift in the name of Elisha.

Then, the unexpected happened…

"And [Elisha] said unto [Gehazi], went not my heart with thee, when [Naaman] turned again from his chariot to meet thee? …"

[Here is the Bigger Question: Elisha asked:]

"Is it a TIME to receive money, and to receive garments, and olive yards, and vineyards, and sheep, and oxen, and menservants, and maidservants?"

After that, came a serious verdict…

The leprosy therefore of Naaman shall cleave unto thee, and unto thy seed forever. And he went out from his presence a leper as white as snow."

- 2 Kings 5:26-27

Elisha scolded Gehazi for that greedy act and told him specifically that "this is not the time to receive gifts," in other words, the time to collect gifts will eventually come if Gehazi will be disciplined enough to wait for it.

Regrettably, Gehazi thought his master was too slow and slack and wasn't taking things as fast as they should. He couldn't wait for the mantle to come properly on him, he wasn't disciplined enough to ignore the gifts that were presented at that moment so he can qualify to enjoy it when the time is right.

Eventually, Gehazi's lack of discipline brought a curse on his entire generation; the leprosy of Naaman was transferred to him and his seed. He lost his place among servants of God; he became slaves to sin and sickness. What a pitiable end!

Another boy became a Prodigal son…

Here is a story to further prove that indiscipline is a terrible time and destiny waster. Another boy could not wait for the right time to receive his inheritance before making rude and urgent demands for it. Interestingly, these were riches that would have been honorably delivered to him if he waited till the time was right.

"And the younger [son] said to his father, Father, give me the portion of goods that falleth to me. And he divided unto them his living.

And not many days after the younger son gathered all together, and took his journey into a far country,

and there wasted his substance with riotous living."

- Luke 15:13

Usually, children are not entitled to the wealth or possessions of their father while he is still alive. But after his death, everyone will be provided portions in the inheritance of their father. Unexpectedly, this particular young man was not going to wait until the death of his father to lay hold on his portion of the inheritance. He went straight to his father one day and demanded his portion in the inheritance.

He was More like someone who wasn't ready to wait for natural processes and appointed times. Surely, he forgot that there is always time for everything under heaven: a time to be born and a time to DIE.

So, the prodigal son took all that he was given and went to a far country. He probably must have seen some of his friends whose parents were wealthy like his father. Maybe he got influenced because they also had taken the same step and are currently enjoying fleeting freedom and vain pleasure far away from home.

The result of that impatience was that the undisciplined boy wasted and lost all that he impatiently acquired. Although, he left home rich but returned poor and wretched. It got so bad that he ate from the food meant for swine not minding the filth all because of the pangs of hunger and consequences of indiscipline.

He would have escaped such unnecessary suffering and torture if he only waited for the right time- the time appointed. How painful are the consequences of indiscipline?

Finally, Absalom wanted David's throne… so bad that he couldn't wait for it

Absalom was the first son of King David; the Bible described him as a 'handsome' man, and a prince who was admired by the entire nation of Israel. Surely, everyone expected that he was supposed to be the next in line as King after David, his father.

"But in all Israel, there was none to be so much praised as Absalom for his beauty: from the sole of his foot even to the crown of his head there was no blemish in him."
- 2 Samuel 14:25

Despite that, Absalom was a great prospect for the throne in Israel; yet he lost his royal chance and died because of gross indiscipline. Unfortunately, Absalom's legitimate and peaceful reign never saw the light of the day. His glory was short-lived by rash decisions that were motivated by pride, malice and lack of self-restraint.

Although, the future looked colorful and promising for the young man; yet, while his father was alive, he gathered men around him and declared himself as king. Absalom stood at the gate of the city and convinced the people that came to see the king turn to him as their new king instead of his father, who was still on the throne.

"And on this manner did Absalom to all Israel that came to the king for judgment: so Absalom stole the hearts of the men of Israel."

- 2 Samuel 15:6

Absalom brewed conspiracy and tried to hijack the kingdom before it would have been right-handed over to him.

"But Absalom sent spies throughout all the tribes of Israel, saying, as soon as ye hear the sound

of the trumpet, then ye shall say, Absalom reigneth in
Hebron."

- 2 Samuel 15:10

Soon, Absalom had the king running for his life away from the palace. He became a 'self-made' king. Most times, when you try to rush into the greatness, you end up becoming an egotistic 'self-made' man, who awaits nothing but sudden ruin in life. Please understand that God is the ultimate maker and lifter of our head. Any attempt to boycott the divine process is always injurious!

Absalom later lost his precious life at the prime of his age. His death was so awful that he hung on a tree and was stabbed to death by Joab, David's Military commander, against the wish of his loving father, who wanted to capture his estranged son.

Sure, greatness will always take some time, process, and steps. Failure to wait for the appointed time may lead to sudden disaster.

"I believe in the process. I believe in four seasons. I believe that winter's tough, but spring's coming. I believe that there's a growing season. And I think that you realize that in life, you grow. You get better."

-Steve Southerland

Indiscipline will make several people miss their time

"Self-discipline is an act of cultivation. It requires you to connect today's actions to tomorrow's results. There's a season for sowing a season for reaping. Self-discipline helps you know which is which."

-Gary Ryan Blair

After several years of struggle, many people eventually miss the time when they would have been easily considered for greater things in life due to acts of indiscipline, negligence, or disobedience.

Consequently, people often abandon their primary assignments and personal responsibilities severally because of lack of personal resolve to stick with the process. This has made people miss great opportunities. Discipline entails or requires that you are found busy with your life goals and assignments.

The bible says in Matthew 24:45-46

"Who then is a faithful and wise servant, whom his lord hath made ruler over his household, to give them meat in due season?

Blessed is that servant whom his Lord shall find him doing so when He comes..." Regardless of what you are going through at the moment, one thing is certain; goodness is on its way for you. However, where will you be when your time of visitation is finally here?

God is looking out for men and women who will diligently wait for their desired change of level, not those that will stray off to frivolities. The bible says, blessed is anyone who is not discouraged or distracted before God eventually shows up on their behalf.

Job said in *"...all the days of my appointed time will I wait, till my change come."* (Job 14:14).

Job was a man who endured difficult trials and temptation. All his seven children and numerous possession were destroyed within a day! Later, his body was attacked with boils that covered him from head to toe. He felt terrible pain and ridicule from friends and even his wife, who told him to curse God and die!

Surely, only a few people have ever been moved to compromise and forsake their integrity like Job. His inner strength was enviable all through the time the suffering. He was ready to reject anything that would cause him to miss the blessings of God that will be his light at the end of the tunnel. He waited patiently for his desired change.

I want you to understand that persistence is key to a successful walk with God. So many hits and run believers are everywhere, while it is still working they are gone already to something else, and their lack of discipline will eventually rule them out of the blessing. No wonder Jesus said, *"Occupy till I come."*

Indiscipline will make a countless number of people to miss rapture because they are not watchful nor careful to observe the times and seasons for the second coming of our savior and king. Don't be like the five foolish virgins, discipline yourself to be counted worthy to partake of the blessings when they are finally here.

"The blessedness of waiting is lost on those who cannot wait, and the fulfillment of the promise is never theirs. They want quick answers to the deepest questions of life and miss the value of those times of anxious waiting, seeking patient uncertainties until the answers come. They lose the moment when the answers are revealed in dazzling clarity."

— Dietrich Bonhoeffer

Finally, indiscipline will Delay you!

Indiscipline can make you delay your progress in life. What you ought to have achieved at the early stage might be prolonged or postponed just because you are not prepared for it.

So, if you cannot wait for your time, you will miss I, and if you miss your time, you have to start all over again. The cycle will continue until you have learned within this wasted period.

Life is about preparation for opportunities. A wise man said, *"luck is when opportunity meets with preparation."* How prepared are you for the blessing, what effort are you making for the desire you need?

When a student fails to discipline himself to attend the lecture and study hard; he or she will fail and delay his year of graduation. The same applies in life; indiscipline has made some miss great opportunities and have to wait at the same level until another season.

"And thou shalt remember all the way which the LORD thy God led thee these forty years in the wilderness, to humble thee, and to prove thee, to know what was in thine heart, whether thou wouldest keep his commandments or no."

-Deuteronomy 8:2 21

The people of Israel were liberated by the mighty hand of God through several miracles and sings that were done by Moses. Yet, they never gave glory to God or keep his commandments; instead, they grumbled and complained at every little discomfort while in the wilderness on their way to the Promised Land.

This gross indiscipline resulted in judgments from God. Their greatest woes and deserved punishment came by suffering, death, and delay.

Finally, if you desire timely breakthroughs and successes in your walk with God and every facet of your life, then, you need to learn to exercise discipline and stop making excuses for your failures and shortcomings.

CHAPTER 3

EXPOSING THE
ENEMIES WITHIN

"So let him who thinks he stands to take heed lest he falls."

-1 Corinthian 10:12

"Know your enemy and know yourself and you can fight a hundred battles
Without disaster. "

-Sun Tzu

These are forces waging war within every single one of us that seeks to put out the light of discipline in diverse areas of our lives. I will let you in on two enemies that need to be dealt with, so we can make progress with developing our inner strength and self-control.

THE ENEMY CALL EGO...

Pride arises as a result of a perceived level of advantage over others. We all need a sense of humility and duty. Jesus Christ washed the feet of his disciples to show that 'servant-hood' and heart of service is not the same as low self-esteem but an expression of humility and leadership which can only be obtained through self-denial and self-discipline.

The bible says,

"Likewise, younger ones be subject to older ones, and all being subject to one another. Put on humility.

For God resists proud ones, but He gives grace to the humble;

Therefore, be humbled under the mighty hand of God, so that He may exalt you in due time,"

-1 Peter 5:5-6

Overcoming a Sense of Perceived Advantage

God has blessed us with diverse and unique opportunities. This should not make us prideful or arrogant. We need to utilize our gifts and privileges to serve people with respect to humbly

King David

King David leveraged on his authority and killed Uriah to cover his sinful act. He wouldn't have done that if he was able to control himself immediately, he found himself in that situation.

"Late one afternoon about dusk, David got up from his couch and was walking around on the roof of

the royal palace. From there, he watched a woman taking a bath, and she was very beautiful to look at. "

-2 Samuel 11:2

Today, indiscipline and lawlessness in the home, workplace, schools, and society are often borne out of an attempt to take advantage of influence over people or affluence in life. Most parents will never discipline their children or ward due to their social status.

King David's children

AMMON, ABSALOM, ADONIJAH were David's sons who will be remembered for several atrocities and regrettable consequences that they suffered just because their father gave them a sense of perceived advantage.

The biblical account of Adonijah's rebellion exposed the consistent error that brought these princes from the throne down to destruction.

The Bible says,

"Meanwhile, about this time Haggith's son Adonijah began to seek a reputation for himself and decided, "I'm going to be king!" So he prepared chariots, cavalry, and 50 soldiers to serve as a security detail to guard him. HIS FATHER HAD NEVER CHALLENGED HIM AT ANY TIME DURING

HIS LIFE BY ASKING HIM, "WHY ARE YOU ACTING LIKE THIS?"

Adonijah was very handsome and had been born after Absalom.

1 Kings 1:5-6

Evidently, Adonijah was a spoilt brat! King David never disciplined or corrected him, so he was prone to presumptuously assume that, even his father's throne belonged to him.

Adonijah's lack of self-control led him straight to rebellion, and this was the beginning of his fall. He was executed for treasonable offenses! What a pitiable end for a promising prince. The perceived advantage became his ruin!

Surely, Adonijah was just one among many other rebellious children. Ammon and Absalom were also disadvantaged despite several opportunities, and just because they abused life's privileges through gross indiscipline.

Ammon raped Tamar, his younger sister right under David's noses. Incest is a grievous expression of indiscipline. Yet, King David never provided moral restraint neither did he punish this abominable offense right after it happened.

However, the first among these princes, Absalom, would not let it slide. Then he took laws into his hands, and Ammon's blood was shed for Tamar's vengeance.

Eventually, Absalom made the first attempt to dethrone King David, and he died in battle against his father's army.

Hophni and Phineas

Eli's children also had a sense of perceived advantage which because of the priesthood. Eli was the High Priest, but his children, Hophni and Phineas were rebellious and callous. They committed several atrocities in the temple against God and His worshipers.

They lacked self-control and were moved by lust and avaricious cravings in the temple, defiling young women and disregarding the offering made to the Most God.

Here is an account of their encounters with people who desire to offer meat offerings to God:

"If the person answered, "Let us do what is right and burn the fat first; then take what you want," the priest's servant [Hophni and Phineas] would say, "No! GIVE IT TO ME NOW! If you don't, I will have to take it by force!"

Eventually, Hophni and Phineas were killed in battle on the same day the noble office of the Priest was permanently taken away from Eli's family.

Apostle Paul did not seize the opportunity he had as a mentor and leader to siphon the people of Thessalonica; rather, he works and shows them how to life and exemplary life. What a foolish thing to do when people think taking advantage of others is the wisest thing to do.

"We did not accept anyone's support without paying for it. Instead, we worked and toiled; we kept working day and night so as not to be an expense to any of you."

-2 Thessalonians 3:8

"There is a kind of elevation which does not depend on fortune; it is a certain air which distinguishes us, and seems to destine us for great things; it is a price which we imperceptibly set upon ourselves."

-Francois de La Rochefoucauld

The enemy called Ease…

"And I will say to my soul, "Soul, you have ample goods laid up for many years; relax, eat, drink, be merry.""

Most people are satisfied and comfortable with their situation so much that they become unaware of possible dangers; some are even oblivious of the changes around them. They feel they have arrived, and there is no more to life than endless enjoyment.

Unfortunately, to be complacent is to be stagnant, and to be stagnant is to slide into retrogression and risk destruction. God is a progressive being who doesn't want us to be complacent with our situation but strive forward every day.

Discipline is needed to win a battle and have a trophy, but it takes greater discipline to retain the trophy. Many people relent after a major victory and eventually lose the trophy cheaply.

"There is, in our nature, a disposition to indulgence, a secret desire to escape from labor, which, unless hourly combated, will overcome and destroy the best faculties of our minds and paralyze our most useful powers."

-Dorothea Dix

An athlete who won a gold medal in an Olympic race must maintain the same level of discipline if he wants to retain the championship medal.

Joshua led Israel to various wars and conquered several kings from the days of Moses until he took over the leadership after his death. God gave Joshua great victories over all their enemies such that his fear was in the heart of kings.

One day, Joshua went to war against a foreign nation, and the battle was fierce and intense. Then, because they haven't conquered the nation by evening, he prayed to God to keep the sun in the sky until the victory is won. Miraculously, his request was granted, and he was victorious.

Interestingly, all these conquests should have been enough to conclude that Joshua had achieved so much so that he needed to settle down and keep dusting his trophy.

However, when Joshua became very old, God spoke to him after many years of great struggles and achievements. The Bible says,

"Now Joshua was old and stricken in years; and the LORD said unto him, thou art old and stricken in years, and THERE REMAINETH YET VERY MUCH LAND TO BE POSSESSED...."

God told Joshua that, there were still more lands to conquer, the succeeding verses listed all the land. This further strengthens the fact that God expects us to be active, diligent, and disciplined all through life.

Certainly, there is no room for complacency; we must consistently battle against thoughts of laying back and do nothing, just because we have achieved something. Many champions have faded away too early because they became complacent.

The bible says,

> *"The slothful man roasteth not that which he took in hunting…"*

-Proverbs 12:27

Also,

> *"A lazy [man or woman] puts his hand in a dish, and he will not return it to his mouth"*

-Proverbs19:24

I want to challenge you to greater works. You must lift your hand to greater victories. Don't rest on your horse there is more to be achieved.

Just as a wise man, Tchaikovsky one said: *"Inspiration is a guest that does not willingly visit the lazy."* Lazy people see the danger in every opportunity while the diligent sees opportunity in every danger.

Finally, Farrah Gray said,

"Comfort is the enemy of achievement."

Therefore, if you desire to find success accomplishments in your walk with God, business, career, and life, then you must recognize the enemies called ego and launch offensive attacks to stop them before they stop you.

CHAPTER 4

DETECT AND MINIMIZE WASTAGE

"When they were all full, he said to his disciples, "Gather the pieces left over; LET US NOT WASTE A BIT."

-John 6:12

Diligence and thoughtfulness are appropriate actions and attitudes that show gratitude for the abundance of divine and natural supply. On the other hand, one of the greatest expression of indiscipline is found with wastage.

This chapter will help you learn how to exercise discipline to detect and minimize wastage in every area of your life. You might have lost several opportunities to be successful in business, career, school, marriage, and life. It is time to reclaim your destiny and stand against wasters.

More so, a lack of inner strength to preserve and utilize resources, relationships, health and time that God released over your life might be causing grievous loses, it is time to harness the power of self-control and provide a beautiful and bright future for yourself and everyone you care about.

Merriam-Webster dictionary defines waste as *"loss of something valuable that occurs because too much of it is being used or because it is being used in a way that is not necessary or effective."*

While Jesus walked this earth, ministering to thousands of people. On the day, he miraculously multiplied five loaves of bread and two fishes to feed five thousand people.

After that, the miracle meal was in excess after every single person in the crowd had been sufficiently fed. The remnants were gathered to avoid wastage. Jesus taught a very great principle by ordering that all the leftovers must be gathered together so that nothing is wasted.

Discipline is taking and owning just what you need per time and avoid wasteful use or abuse of any blessing. We live in a generation where a lot of people are caught in the web of competition; they spend lavishly over stuff just because it is in vogue not because they need it.

Some lack the discipline to take care of what they presently own simply because they have the excess money to acquire more in excess. The weight of diverse waste generated in most cities is enough to reduce the level of poverty in other parts of the world if they are judiciously recycled, managed and distributed.

More so, abundance always comes with responsibility. Exercising self-control when it comes to managing your resources is crucial to preserving God's blessings over your life. No wonder why, an attitude of wastage has limited the blessing of God over a lot of people because God is not sure if they will use and spread the resources to give Him glory.

You need diligence to detect and minimize waste

"He also that is slothful in his work is a brother to him that is a great waster."

- Proverbs 18:9

Laziness breeds wastefulness. A slothful individual is the same as a GREAT waster. In other words, even when someone works hard to acquire certain things; yet, if he wastes them, the lot of the lazy man will eventually be his lot in life. Wastefulness always engenders poverty.

Here are a few kinds of wasters that must be evicted from any life. Except your life is guarded against these wasters; you have so much work to be done.

There are wasters of destinies

Excessive Social media and other forms of Entertainment

Today, social media and many other modes of communication, technology, and entertainment can be a blessing or a curse, depending on how we use them and not be subjugated to be ruled by these things. Some people have no business launching or joining some social media platforms because it won't add any value to them.

While some use social media to their advantage as a medium to advertise their product and services, others waste their precious time watching, grumbling, wishing, and waning online.

The web has caught several young people, and a huge chunk of their lives and livelihood are being wasted every day. A lot of money is wasted for internet data subscriptions simply to admire people's pictures, watch entertainment, or play video games. Some of these things are not bad when they are done with self-control; however, the reverse is often the case when we allow internet, social media and entertainment put a leech on us to control and hold us back from doing things that will move our lives forward.

Mind the kind of people you hang around (toxic relationships)

There are friends, families and associates who add good and valuable things to your life. They add knowledge, experiences, material, fame, and above all and spiritual progress to your life.

Also, there are subtractive, toxic, and wasteful friends who add no value or significant natural and spiritual progress to your life. They cause rancor, disaffection, competition, and chaos in your life. They are busy but not productive. They take from you but don't replenish. They are there to grow the bad in you and kill the good inside of you. Surely, the kind of company you keep determines what accompanies you in life.

"He who walks with the wise shall be wise, but a companion with fools shall be destroyed."

-Proverbs 13:20

It takes discipline to evaluate objectively and critically examine the kinds of 32 relationships in your life. Have you discovered people in your life who significantly influence the way you think, your perspective about issues and life generally.

This is why, if you keep company with wasters, you end up being a typical waster.

"A man who dares to waste one hour has not discovered the value of life."

-Charles Darwin

So, you need to stand and play by your own rules

Human wants are insatiable. You cannot please everyone either can you satisfy the need or desire of everybody that comes to your way. Any attempt to please everyone is signing-in for frustration. So do what you can and leave the rest. Let people know you for who you are, you don't have to be everything to everyone, be disciplined enough to say "No!" when you should.

In conclusion, you need to be disciplined enough to take time out and evaluate your life so you can detect, minimize, or obliterate wasters, clutters in it. Find limiting habits, people, gadgets, social media accounts, and several other hindrances in your life and make adjustments where necessary. God bless you

CHAPTER 5

KEEP YOUR
EYES ON THE PRIZE

"*Let your eyes look directly ahead and let your gaze be fixed straight in front of you.*"

-Proverbs 4:25

Nothing builds inner strength, courage, and power beyond the influence of a vision. The moment light has dawned on an aspect of your life; then you are sensitized to make clear and strong decisions and stick convincingly by them.

Surely, distractions, pleasures, and disasters can come against your spiritual, moral and natural resolve to raise and keep higher standards in your work, family, career, and life; however, a sense of vision will keep you from slipping off the golden track.

This chapter will help you find reasons to consistently commit yourself to the goals, objectives, and assignments in your life. You will learn how to envision the good outcome so vividly that you become motivated to endure, persist, and strive towards the great things that lie ahead of you.

First, you need a vision…find it!

"And Jehovah answered me and said, Write the vision, and make it plain on the tablets, that he who reads it may run; for the vision is still for an appointed time, but it speaks to the end, and it does not lie. Though it lingers, wait for it; because it will surely come. It will not tarry."

-Habakkuk 2:2-3

Our focus determines perception, and our perception will eventually determine how we make progress in diverse areas of life. No one ever wins the prize without consistently setting his yes on it. What focusing on the prize does is to give us the energy to win and resolve not to compete.

There is always something better ahead

"Brethren, I do not regard myself as having laid hold of it yet; but one thing I do: forgetting what lies behind and reaching forward to what lies ahead; I press on toward the goal for the prize of the upward call of God in Christ Jesus."

- Philippians 3:13-14

Apostle Paul was one of the greatest Apostle in his days and Author of about 75% of the books of the

New Testament. His record is nearly unparalleled, despite his incongruous and Anti-Christianity background.

It is amazing to find a man of tremendous success in life and ministry still able to say that, his past successes are nothing compared with the prize that is set before him. This is interesting.

I want to let you know that there is always something bigger ahead. The moment anyone ceases to strive for the prize of an upward and higher call then, they relapse to mediocrity, slothfulness and indiscipline.

Surely, there are distractions

"Successful people maintain a positive focus in life no matter what is going on around them. They stay focused on their past successes rather than their past failures, and on the next action steps they need to take to get them closer to the fulfillment of their goals rather than all the other distractions that life presents to them."

-Jack Canfield

Be conscious of the kind of information you receive into your mind. The mind is the battle-field for focus and appropriate evaluation of the task ahead.

You must continually savor the sweetness of your tomorrow so; you can endure the sour taste of today's experiences.

Certainly, there will be other things in life that may appear to look better than the great things that formed your original goals, vision, and mission for your 36 life; yet, you must reject these distractions and seemingly better alternatives if you must make out something significant with your life.

There are no short cuts

"There is a pathway that seems right to a man, but in the end, it's a road to death."

-Proverbs 14:12

It takes discipline to stop making excuses for taking your eyes off the track. You must cease from trying to get things done using compromising alternatives. There have never been any genuine short-cuts to breakthrough or success, but there are many short cuts to failures and frustrations.

Angela Duckworth one said, "there is no short cut to through excellence." It is far better to be slow and steady and get to the pinnacle of success in life than to be in haste and miss the purpose of God.

God Bless You!

CHAPTER 6

WHEN THE GOING GETS TOUGH

"Most of the important things in the world have been accomplished by people who had kept on trying when there seemed to be no hope at all."

-Dale Carnegie

" I have set the Lord always before me. Because he is at my right hand, I will not be shaken."

-Psalm 16:8

Have a thick skin

For most people, life has never been a bed of roses. Trial and challenges are inevitable on the rugged road to greatness. Every man and woman will be tested for patience in adversity and character in prosperity.

Why should you stay down because you were pushed aside by frustration and struck down by failure? You need to realize that disappointments are part of the package for every success story. **The spark of passion is found in trying times.**

People may promise to help you, and then fail to do so, but never lose your nerve. Greater help and endless possibilities reside in you! Disciple and self-control will reveal your inner-power.

Your loved ones may dissert you when you needed love and validation; yet, don't sink in the mire of depression or wallow in self-subjugation. Rise above your situation because what you are going through is just a phase and season, not the end of your journey to greatness.

Without a doubt, rewards may seem farther from you coming after many years of dedication and commitment to a particular project, discipline, practice, or exercise. All I have to say to you is; keep on moving on. Surely, there is light at the end of that tunnel.

> *"When the going gets tough, the tough gets going."*
>
> —Joseph Kennedy

JOSEPH A HERO OF DISCIPLINE EVEN IN HARD TIMES...

I want to let you in on the life of an exemplary leader and master of self-control. Joseph was a man of character and inner strength. When you examine the story of his life as narrated in the book of Genesis; you will easily conclude that he was like Gold forged out of the flames of adversity and episodes of suffering.

He began as a loved son with his father Jacob before envy drove his brother to sell him off as a slave to Potiphar, who became his slave master for many years. This was not the end!

Later in Joseph's life, everything seemed great and promising, he was put in charge of everything in his master's household because he exemplified integrity, character, and responsibility.

While Joseph rose through the ranks in Potiphar's house, his master's wife ceaselessly seduced him. She attempted to tear off Joseph's armor of character and self-restraint. However, she only tore his cloth.

Eventually, Joseph was sent to prison, but that was not the end! Most of the remaining chapters of this book will expose and explain certain truths about the enviable life of Joseph.

He became the Prime Minister of Egypt and the man who was saddled with global food distribution and humanitarian intervention project during seven years of worldwide famine. This was a phenomenal outcome after everything seemed over for Joseph, personal commitment to excellence and character always provided him with victory and access to new heights. You too can be great...regardless of what had happened or is happening in your life.

Believe you were born to win

"And [Joseph] dreamed yet another dream, and told it his brethren, and said, Behold, I have dreamed a dream more; and, behold, the sun and the moon and the eleven stars made obeisance to me."

-Genesis 37:9

When Joseph was still with his father, he kept having dreams that pointed to the fact that he will become a powerful, prominent, and influential individual. Joseph became aware of his 39 leadership heritage and inherent gifts at a very early age. This awareness progressed to birth a sense of personal responsibility, deep character, and inner strength in him.

Eventually, Joseph was hated and persecuted because he dared to dream bigger than others, even his father and mother.

However, there are no mountains too high or valleys too deep or oceans too wide that inner strength and personal conviction cannot triumph. Everything is possible for everyone who believes.

This means that, when you are faced with daunting situations, your faith in who you truly are will help you maintain higher standards of discipline and self-control.

For Joseph, a sense of purpose for his life became an anchor in trouble and motivation for victory over temptations and trials. He walked and worked in the dark, not alone but with the flames of a lively hope.

Keep hope alive…Expect to win

"Let's not get tired of doing what is good, for at the right time we will reap a harvest—if we do not give up."

-Galatians 6:9

"And the LORD was with Joseph, and he was a prosperous man, and he was in the house of his master the Egyptian."

-Genesis 39:2

Joseph became a prosperous man even as a slave in Potiphar's house. This should encourage everyone who feels like giving up. I want to let you know that you can prosper even in the most challenging situations. You should not be defined by what your predicaments. You need to rise above the pain and take responsibility for your life.

"You may encounter many defeats, but you must not be defeated. It may be necessary to encounter the defeats, so you can know who you are, what you can rise from, how you can still come out of it."

—Maya Angelou

My friend, it does not matter whether you are flying or walking. What matter most is that you are not stagnant or giving up. After every injustice and difficult experience, Troubles often come into our lives to make us feel like doing the right thing is a waste of time. These are times when we miss the chance to prove the strength and power of resolve, hope, and character that lies within us.

Therefore, have you been knocked down, rise! I challenge you to shake off every challenges and discouragement that may seek to paralyze or stop you before you make it through. Expect that you are almost there and you will surely get there.

A wise man once said, *"Winners never quit, and quitters never win".* The major difference between the winner and the loser is the winner see the picture of victory and celebration in any difficult situation while the loser sees only the problems.

Hope says, hang on to your dreams, your faithfulness, and your integrity. Self-control, when things get tough, is like a light that in your darkest hour; surely you will overcome.

"When you come to the end of your rope, tie a knot and hang on."

-Franklin D. Roosevelt

CHAPTER 7

LEVERAGE ON DIVINE ADVANTAGE

"What you endure disciplines you: God is treating you as sons. Is there a son whom his father does not discipline?"

-Hebrews 12:7

Discipline requires so much exercise, inner strength, practice, and endurance. More so, true and complete obedience must be attained only through the help of the Holy Spirit. We cannot make moral, spiritual, and natural progress without God.

Therefore, we need to discover and leverage on divine advantage. To do this, we need to realize that:

God is with us, and He is interested in our success in life...

The presence of God is a soothing assurance and comforting awareness to everyone who believes. Doing life alone without God can be boring and difficult. There must be a way to supernaturally secure assistance for all that we need to do in life.

Also, one of the last assurance that Jesus gave His disciples before He ascended was that He will always be with them even to the end. This, for me, is the greatest promise for any believer.

The confidence of a little child is enhanced when the parents are around him. He can rest safe and secured in the presence of the parent. In Deuteronomy 31:6, Moses spoke confidence into the children of Israel by letting them know that God will not leave them or abandon them.

"Be strong and courageous. Don't fear or tremble before them, because the LORD your God will be the One who keeps on walking with you—

He won't leave you or abandon you." From the verse we see also that assurance and awareness of divine presence makes a man strong and courageous, just like a baby with his dad. An assurance of divine presence takes away fear, and this becomes possible because you know there is no situation that God cannot handle. All power in heaven and on earth is given to Him.

"What shall we then say to these things? If God is for us, who can be against us?

Finally, as you strive to live a disciplined life; you need to realize that God's presence promises supernatural access to divine help. Surely, you will face diverse temptations to give up and compromise. You must know that God is available to help you, and your attitude to this gesture is to remain steadfast and be disciplined enough to keep his instruction as he has said: "if you are willing and obedient, you shall eat the fruit of the land."

Be sensitive to his voice

"Be still, and know that I am God! I will be praised among the nations; I will be praised in the earth."

-Psalm 46:10

For someone embarking on a journey, especially in unfamiliar terrain, the use of a compass or a human guide is essential if he must arrive at his destination safely. So, in the journey of life, God's leading through His voice is very important. The majestic voice of God was all that confidently led Abram from his father's house to a land that God promised to give him. God didn't tell him all that he will go through, but at every step of the way, God spoke and showed him the next step after following his voice in doing what was previously commanded.

Honestly, the world is crowded with noise and life circumstance; it takes discipline and the Holy Spirit to discern the voice of God among the multitude of thought that run through our mind every day. Sometimes our situations may appear gloomy, but we have not heard the truth our circumstances until we heard from God. Discipline will keep our ears open to the voice of God irrespective of the voices from outside.

Develops the fruit of the spirit

But the fruit of the Spirit is love, joy, peace, longsuffering, gentleness, goodness, faith, Meekness, temperance: against such, there is no law.

- Galatians 5:22-23

When the Pharisees came to the baptism of John as recorded in Matthew 3, the Bibles says John the Baptist told them to bring forth fruits worthy of repentance. It is the fruit that a tree bears that determines its worth. So also the fruits of the spirit are not behaviors but a lifestyle, the normal behavior of a believer, and it takes discipline because there are times your patience will be tested, there are period loving people may be out of place but yet you have to. The fruit of the Spirit is said to be the working of the Holy Spirit in the life of a believer, so it's beyond determination but supernatural enablement.

Be filled with the word of God

"As newborn babes, desire the sincere milk of the word that ye may grow thereby:"

-Peter 2:2

It's all about been filled with the word of God. How much of the word you know determines how much it will reflect in your life, no one can live what he does not know about. Peter admonished that we should desire the word of God just like a baby will cry out to express his desire for milk. Among many other things, the word of God is needed for our spiritual growth, just like there is no alternative for milk in the growth of a baby. And our spiritual growth determines the level of dominion we command.

"Thy word have I hid in mine heart, that I might not sin against thee. "

- Psalms 119:11

Another reason to feed and be filled with the word of God that it purifies our life and teaches us how to live right. The society and the devil won't deceive you.

But it takes discipline to feed on the word, let alone been filled with it. Sitting down with the word daily takes discipline, but the effect is unmatchable.

Be accountable

"Confess your faults one to another, and pray one for another, that ye may be healed. The effectual fervent prayer of a righteous man availeth much."

-James 5:16

Accountability helps to put one in check, thereby reducing error. It eradicates the time and energy you expend on distracting events and other unproductive performance or behavior. It will stir you up every morning with the sense of feeling that you have to give an account of how you spend every dime of your day. So, accountability is the hallmark of responsibility, which can only be attained with self-discipline and diligent. When you are not accountable to God and yourself, it is impossible to be accountable to and for others. Several sleazes committed today to arise due to lack of accountability to oneself.

Paul knew the importance of accountability when he admonished us to confess our fault one to another so we can receive help. Where you are weak, another is strong. Nobody is created to leave in isolation, exclusively from fellow. Brethren we are made to succeed with people. When you are struggling, due accountability helps to strengthen our discipline.

CONCLUSION

So far, I believe you have been inspired with all the dimension of discipline as learned in this book. No individual advances beyond the level of their disciplined life they are willing to live. Where your discipline stops, that's where your color stops. The sun, for instance, does not shine when it feels like, there is a stipulated time by God for the sun to rise and set and it does. Discipline is doing what is expected of you, not what you feel like doing. So it's important to go from here and begin to note your expectations in your walk with God, in your career, business, among others to emerge an excellent personality.

Finally, where you are today and what you have become is a function of the discipline of yesterday, so also where you desire to be tomorrow will largely depend on the discipline you are willing to live by.

God bless you!

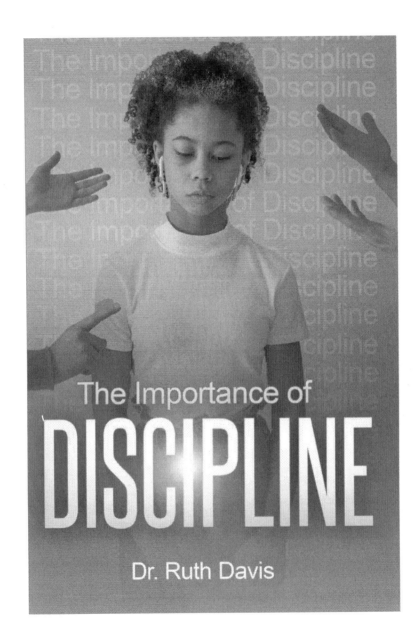

The Importance of
DISCIPLINE

Dr. Ruth Davis

Made in the USA
Middletown, DE
18 March 2022

62776847R00043